WOMEN
PRAY
FOR MEN

Mikala Smith

◆ FriesenPress

Suite 300 - 990 Fort St
Victoria, BC, V8V 3K2
Canada

www.friesenpress.com

ISBN
978-1-5255-3557-4 (Hardcover)
978-1-5255-3558-1 (Paperback)
978-1-5255-3559-8 (eBook)

1. RELIGION, CHRISTIAN LIFE, PRAYER

Distributed to the trade by The Ingram Book Company

Table of Contents

Preface

I have it on my heart to pray for men all month (January 2017), coincidence that in this same month the Women's March on Washington happened? I think not![1] Cover the men, call out God destiny over them, not who they are now, but who God says they are. Pray against division of the women and men; pray for unity and teamwork.

These prayers are for ALL men! We all have men in our lives: husbands, sons, fathers, grandpas, uncles, nephews,

---

[1] "On November 9, 2016, the day after Donald Trump was elected President of the United States, in reaction to Trump's election campaign and political views, and his defeat of female presidential nominee Hillary Clinton, Teresa Shook of Hawaii created a Facebook event and invited friends to march on Washington in protest.

The **Women's March** was a worldwide protest on January 21, 2017, to advocate legislation and policies regarding human rights and other issues, including women's rights, immigration reform, healthcare reform, reproductive rights, the natural environment, LGBTQ rights, racial equality, freedom of religion, and workers' rights. Most of the rallies were aimed at Donald Trump, immediately following his inauguration as President of the United States, largely due to statements that he had made and his positions which were regarded by many as anti-women or otherwise offensive. "

2017 Women's March; Wikipedia The Free Encyclopedia; Wikimedia Foundation, INC.; https://en.wikipedia.org/wiki/2017_Women%27s_March. August 5, 20018.

cousins, students, co-workers, neighbours and political leaders, among others.

I believe in the power of prayer, as **James 5:16, KJV** states, "The effectual fervent prayer of a righteous man availeth much". What would happen if the people alive in this generation invested time into praying for each other? There would be a ripple effect into society. So, I present before you the challenge: will you commit to pray for men? If not you, then who?

This book is more than just a good read or another to check off your list. It is a starting point for the Holy Spirit to stir within you your own prayers. It is full of deliberate prayer actions: compilations of prayers, songs, Bible verses, blank pages to write out your own prayers or to take notes. This book is designed to be interactive: write your prayers out, speak them out, sing them out in declarations and look up the songs. Throughout the prayers I offer here, there are blank spaces, which are for you to insert the specific male you are praying for; you can write in their name(s) or leave it blank, as this book is designed to be used continually throughout your life to cover different men for different seasons of your life and theirs. You might spend one year on a specific grandpa and the next year on another family relative. You might use it to pray for your husband and when you have a son use it to pray for him too. You might dedicate a specific topic to one neighbour who you know is struggling with something and another topic over a friend who is struggling in another area.

This book is not the end all be all, it is a starting point to help you become inspired and grow passionate about praying for men. If you do not have the words to pray, you can stand in agreement with the prayers I have shared. I strongly encourage you to not passively just read the book from cover to cover, but to go through the process, over and over and over again until it sinks in your heart that God is for the men and he is for you too. Take the time and meditate; ask God to show you areas to pray over the men in your life.

My intention is that you are blessed and the Holy Spirit fills you with peace, love and compassion as you actively go through each area of covering the men in prayer.

Happy praying, Mikala Smith

Introduction: Women Pray for Men

Pray for the men, oh the Lord said, "**Pray for the Men**"! Cover the men in prayer all you mighty women of God, cover the men in this hour and keep covering them! Men and women be unified by the spirit of the Lord. Do not abandon the men; do not talk poorly of man; remember God created them and thus, you speak poorly of God the creator. Stand up and pray for the men. Who will stand and pray for the men in this hour? Who will stand in the gap of women and men and bring unity? "You judge the man, but you are not a man, you do not understand, if you want them to change you need to start praying for them, for I am God and I work mightily through prayer," says the Lord. Stop talking, gossiping, slandering and belittling (that is too easy). Who will take the challenge and start praying for the men?

I dare you to pray and watch what God does. Pray for men when you do not feel like it, pray when it does not make sense, pray when you would rather give up on them, pray when they make you cry, pray when you cannot trust them. Pray, pray and pray. Who will commit to pray for the men? Keep praying and when you do not see change, keep praying and when you still do not see change, keep praying. Who will pray for the men, not for one day, not a week, not a month, not six months, not a year, not five, ten or fifteen years, but for a lifetime. I dare you to pray and watch as God will move not only on the men's hearts, but the women's hearts also and when you do start seeing change, **KEEP PRAYING**!

Women, if you want men to step up in the Church and leadership, start praying for the men.

Women, if you want men to be godly fathers, husbands, sons, etc., start praying for the men.

Women, if you want men to not be lazy and be providers, start praying for the men.

Women, if you want men to burn with passion and to chase after God, start praying for the men.

Women, if you want men to not abandon their families, start praying for the men.

Women, if you want men to not abuse substances or have addictions, start praying for the men.

Women, if you want men to be trustworthy, honest and honourable, start praying for the men.

Women, if you want men to not live by lustful and fleshly desires, start praying for the men.

Women, if you want men to not shut down and close off and fall into isolation and depression, start praying for the men.

Women, if you want men to not be afraid of commitment, but to commit to marriage, start praying for the men.

Below you can insert your personal wants from men and be assured that by praying through these wants the Holy Spirit will either change that man's heart or your heart or both hearts concerning the want. God is for you and he is also for the men for whom you pray.

Women, if you want men to _____, start praying for the men.

Women, you want men not to _____, start praying for the men.

Women, you want men not to _____, start praying for the men.

<u>We are going back to the first book; Genesis, where men and women are a team!</u>

Genesis 2:18, NIV

The Lord God said, "It is not good for the man to be alone. I will make a **helper** suitable for him."

Genesis 2:20–24, NIV

. . . But for Adam no suitable helper was found. [21]So the Lord God caused the man to fall into a deep sleep; and while he was sleeping, he took one of the man's ribs and then closed up the place with flesh. [22] Then the Lord God made a woman from the rib he had taken out of the man, and he brought her to the man.

[23]The man said,

"This is now bone of my bones
and flesh of my flesh;
she shall be called 'woman,'
for she was taken out of man."

[24]That is why a man leaves his father and mother and is united to his wife, and they become one flesh.

Genesis 1:27–31, NIV

[27]So God created mankind in his own image,
in the image of God he created them;
male and **female** he created **them**.

[28]God blessed **them** and said to **them**, "Be fruitful and increase in number; fill the earth and subdue

it. Rule over the fish in the sea and the birds in the sky and over every living creature that moves on the ground."

[29]Then God said, "I give you every seed-bearing plant on the face of the whole earth and every tree that has fruit with seed in it. They will be yours for food. [30]And to all the beasts of the earth and all the birds in the sky and all the creatures that move along the ground—everything that has the breath of life in it—I give every green plant for food." And it was so. [31] God saw all that he had made, and it was **very good.**

<u>Unity commands a blessing from God!</u>

Psalm 133, NIV

[1]How good and pleasant it is
when God's people live together in unity!
[2]It is like precious oil poured on the head,
running down on the beard,
running down on Aaron's beard,
down on the collar of his robe.
[3]It is as if the dew of Hermon
were falling on Mount Zion.
For there the Lord bestows his blessing,
even life forevermore.

Pray for the Women

Prayer of agreement:

I pray for the women during the months and years that they pray for the men. I come in agreement and stand against any attacks of the enemy that would plant seeds of strife and division into any relationship. I declare a protection over these praying women's hearts (spirits), minds (thoughts) and souls (emotions) as they cover the men in prayer. I pray against any bitterness, envy or hatred that has gripped at these women's hearts in the past towards men, in the present towards men or prevention from the future towards men. We come humbly and honoured with the privilege to cover men in prayer. Give women the Holy Spirit to see men with the same eyes as Jesus sees them and hearts to love these men the way Jesus loves them. As women pray, help us continually to discern our heart's motives towards the men. Our prayers are not to fix what we deem to be a problem with men; we will not see men as a problem to fix, they are not a problem to fix, but we women join alongside and stand in unison with the men.

Keep our hearts and motives pure during our prayers and give us revelation to the areas of our hearts and minds that need to be changed and softened towards these men. We pray for extra grace as we guard our hearts from any issues in us that come up as we cover the men. "**Keep thy heart with all diligence; for out of it are the issues of life,**" **Proverbs 4:23, KJV.**

Let our thoughts as women align with your thoughts of men, God, in Jesus' name, Amen!

Philippians 4:8, KJV

[8]Finally, brethren, whatsoever things are true, whatsoever things are honest, whatsoever things are just, whatsoever things are pure, whatsoever things are lovely, whatsoever things are of good report; if there be any virtue, and if there be any praise, think on these things.

Pray to Soften Men's Hearts

Prayer:

I pray for _____ heart to be softening. I pray that you, Lord, would start to massage his heart, that all hardness has to flee as you are massaging his heart. I pray for walls that were built out of hurt, insecurity and rejection would start to crumble. That _____ would be able to open up and be vulnerable. I pray that _____ strength would be found in you and not by building up walls of protection.

Pray/sing the lyrics from the album *West of Here-Kingdoms*[2] over _____; be intentional, you are not just singing a good song, but actually making declarations over _____.

---

2 West of Here-Kingdoms; YouTube; https://www.youtube.com/watch?v=nTymaRTfKPo. Published on March 4, 2016

Note: West of Here is a local Edmonton, Canada band. *West of Here-Kingdoms* can be purchased from westofhereband.com

Prayer:

I pray for all closed -off hearts that have manifested in men's lives as fear, depression, isolation and anxiety to be broken off in Jesus' name. I confess over _____ heart that it is healthy, whole and able to make healthy connections and overflow with love for others.

Oh, I thank you Jesus that you are massaging the men's heart in this hour, in this month and in this year, I thank you that this will be a year where _____ heart is soften. I declare that Jesus is massaging hearts, oh yes, Jesus is massaging hearts, Jesus is massaging to soften men's hearts. Where the blood (representation of life giving and love) has been blocked, Jesus is massaging it; blockages are being removed and the blood is flowing freely.

I even speak that as men's hearts are being healed of deep emotional wounds that this would cause a healing in the physical, where these emotional heart wounds have manifested in the natural as . . .

Heart attacks,
Angina,
Arrhythmia,
Atherosclerosis,
Atrial fibrillation,
Cardiac arrest,
Cardiomyopathy,

Congenital heart disease,
Coronary artery disease,
Enlarged heart,
Heart block,
Heart failure,
Infective (bacterial) endocarditis,
Inherited rhythm disorders,
Kawasaki disease,
Marfan syndrome,
Pericarditis,
Rheumatic heart disease,
Valve disorders,
etc.

... that the men's bill of health would be cleared in Jesus' name and the enemy has no dominion over their hearts. I am praying for miracles in the men's emotional and physical state of their hearts. I see healthy hearts, I see healthy hearts and I see healthy men's hearts.

If you know of a specific heart condition, either one listed above or another one, that has manifested in _____, pray over him in your own words and believe in God's healing power to touch him.

Pray for the Future Husbands

Prayer:

As a single woman I pray for my future husband. I thank God that when the timing is right God will unify us as a couple. God, my husband and I will be braided together like a triple-braided cord, carrying much strength and unity in the realm of Christian marriages. "A person standing alone can be attacked and defeated, but two can stand back-to-back and conquer. Three are even better, for a triple-braided cord is not easily broken," **Ecclesiastes 4:12, NLT.** I thank you God that I have been set-aside for my husband and he has been set-aside for me. I thank you God that you are awaking my future husband's desires to be married and are directing him in choosing a godly women with whom he will be equally yoked. I pray where there has been any hopelessness, rejection, hurt, fear of getting it wrong (mostly due to witnessing and living through divorces and unhealthy marriages) and a spirit of independence, that you are realigning my future husband's thoughts and actions with the word of the Lord concerning marriage, as **Proverbs 18:22, NLT** states, "The man who finds a wife finds a treasure and he receives favor from the LORD". I thank you that you are protecting my future husband's heart and emotions from entering into deceptive relationships. "Charm is deceptive, and beauty is fleeting; but a woman who fears the LORD is to be praised," **Proverbs 31:30, NIV.** I thank you that my husband does not fall prey to lusts of the flesh, immoral sexual acts, or pornography and thus inhibit him from wanting a real life partner (not a fantasy) and being fenced into the quick gratifications of sin that acts as a pacifier to temporal loneliness. I thank you that our marriage will glorify you and bring honour and respect back to the sacredness of the union between a man and a woman. I thank you that my husband seeks you first in all his ways and understandings and is continuously building godly character. I thank you that you have surrounded him with wise, godly counsel from wise, married, Christian couples, pastors and leaders, who can openly speak and give sound advice and judgement in the area of marriage and I thank you that my future husband has ears to hear and a heart open to receive.

I call forth the future godly husbands to be awakened in this hour. I decree that they are mighty, valiant men, ready to take their rightful positions as leaders of the family unit and Church. I decree that the single women will start to be pursued by their future husbands as God has purposed.

Scales are falling off of the future husband's eyes and their eyes are being opened and hearts softened towards their future brides. God is ordaining the future husband's steps to cross and align with their future brides. I declare no more delays, no more delays and no more delays on the manifestation of these godly unions on earth; these godly unions will represent the most precious wedding of them all for eternity, **Jesus with his bride, the Church**.

Pray for the Current Husbands

I see a pillar (like a Greek column) representing the husband holding up his family; however, this pillar (husband) has to be on a sturdy foundation (God) and not have cracks in it (thoughts, lies and habits that do not line up with God's best and Biblical truth in their lives), otherwise the pillars and the entire structure (family) will be prone to collapsing. This vision quickens to my remembrance and probably yours to the parable in **Matthew 7:24–27, ESV**, Build Your House on the Rock:

²⁴ Everyone then who hears these words of mine and does them will be like a wise man who built his house on the rock. ²⁵ And the rain fell, and the floods came, and the winds blew and beat on that house, but it did not fall, because it had been founded on the rock. ²⁶And everyone who hears these words of mine and does not do them will be like a foolish man who built his house on the sand. ²⁷ And the rain fell, and the floods came, and the winds blew and beat against that house, and it fell, and great was the fall of it.

Let this be our husband's heart's cry . . .

Joshua 24:15, NIV

But as for me and my family, we will serve the Lord.

I have it on my heart to pray for husbands who are not Christians. I am not insensitive to the fact that not every Christian woman's husband is a believer, whether you chose to marry a non-believer, you became a believer after you were married, or your husband has backslid. I still decree over them a godly future, not trying to fix something that you think is broken, but loving them where they are at and seeing them the way Jesus sees them . . . because God is outside of time. God sees their future, so begin decreeing out over them who and what God says about them as a husband, even if you do not see it yet with your natural eyes.

Pray for the Current and Future Sons

Pray over your current son(s) or future son(s); the following scriptures are declarations you can continually make pertaining to your sons. At the end of this section there is a specific prayer for if you do not have any sons.

Prayer:

I thank you *before conception* for my son and bring to remembrance:

Jeremiah 1:5, NIV

Before I formed you in the womb I knew you, before you were born I set you apart; I appointed you as a prophet to the nations.

I thank you *after conception* for my son and bring to remembrance:

Psalm 139:13–18, NASB

¹³For You formed my inward parts; You wove me in my mother's womb. ¹⁴ I will give thanks to You, for I am fearfully and wonderfully made; Wonderful are Your works, And my soul knows it very well ¹⁵ My frame was not hidden from You, When I was made in secret, And skilfully wrought in the depths of the earth,¹⁶Your eyes have seen my unformed substance; And in Your book were all written The days that were ordained for me, When as yet there was not one of them. ¹⁷How precious also are Your thoughts to me, O God! How vast is the sum of them! ¹⁸If I should count them, they would outnumber the sand.

I thank you after birth when my son is a **baby**:

I dedicate my son(s) to God just like Hannah did with Samuel, **1 Samuel 1:1–28**. I thank you for healthy baby boys who grow up knowing God so intimately that nothing could ever tear them away from loving and serving God.

I thank you for my son when he is a **child**:

My son will know the word and character of God. Just like Joshua:

Joshua 1:7–9, ESV

[7]Only be strong and very courageous; be careful to do according to all the law which Moses My servant commanded you; do not turn from it to the right or to the left, so that you may have success wherever you go. [8]"This book of the law shall not depart from your mouth, but you shall meditate on it day and night, so that you may be careful to do according to all that is written in it; for then you will make your way prosper, and then you will have success. [9]"Have I not commanded you? Be strong and courageous! Do not tremble or be dismayed, for the LORD your God is with you wherever you go.

I thank you for my son when he is a *teenager*:

I thank you that God has bestowed wisdom on him and he will not be snared by the evil one into temptations, but walk in great wisdom in every area such as Solomon:

1 Kings 29–30, NASB

[29]Now God gave Solomon wisdom and very great discernment and breadth of mind, like the sand that is on the seashore. [30]Solomon's wisdom surpassed the wisdom of all the sons of the east and all the wisdom of Egypt.

I thank you for my son when he is an *adult*:

Just like in **John 15:14–16**, my son is a friend of Jesus because he obeys his commands and my son will bear much fruit for the Lord.

John 15:14–16, NIV

¹⁴ You are my friends if you do what I command. ¹⁵I no longer call you servants, because a servant does not know his master's business. Instead, I have called you friends, for everything that I learned from my Father I have made known to you. ¹⁶ You did not choose me, but I chose you and appointed you so that you might go and bear fruit—fruit that will last— and so that whatever you ask in my name the Father will give you.

Still pray over all the sons in this world:

Even if you have not biologically given birth to a son, still pray for all the sons of the world, as these sons will one day become men imprinting society from within their spheres of influence: occupations and become future son-in-laws, brother-in-laws, cousins, friends, leaders, pastors, role models and colleagues. Or maybe you are in a position of authority over sons of this world, a teacher, counsellor, coach, youth pastor, Sunday school teacher, music teacher, child care worker, employer, or mentor and you are faced with the many challenges of having a positive influence over these sons as the worldly systems seem to be in the majority of opposition to positive influences. Or maybe your heart simply cries for the sons of this world.

Prayer:

I thank you for all of God's sons, even if they are not my biological sons. I thank you God that you hear my heart's cry and burden over the raising up of godly sons of this world into godly men. I declare where any son has felt abandoned and unloved in the natural world that you are covering and having grace over this son in the spiritual. I thank you that from this day forward _____ will feel the love of you, Abba. I speak protection and love over _____. I thank you that as _____ journeys throughout life into adulthood that his steps are being marked carefully by you. I bind up any attack from the enemy over the moral decay of the sons of this world. I speak to any damaged spirit of any son that has taken away from their innocence; we claim freedom over them to be set free as a son of God.

Pray for Men's Boldness, Strength and Courage

It takes boldness, strength and courage to be a man. It is in a man's make-up to be a leader, conqueror, protector and provider and not show weakness. However, men have a lot of pressure to keep up a façade that is nearly impossible by their own strength because they were never expected to do so on their own strength but by cleaving to Jesus' strength. Applying only their own strength, the façade can only last so long before something has to give, often leading to abuse, depression, anxiety, isolation and escapism through addictions to drugs, alcoholism, sports, sex, porn and gambling, among others.

The enemy is attacking men's identity including the boldness, strength and courage given to them. I pray against the enemies attack on male identity (identity will be covered later on in the book).

Prayer:

I pray for _____ to be full of the boldness, strength and courage of the Lion of Judah in him. I pray that the sleeping Lion will be woken up inside of him and start to roar passionately out of his innermost being. I pray that _____ would not cower down in the face of the pressures of work, finances, relationships, parenting and chores, but would face them head on with boldness, strength and courage. Oh, I call forth the sleeping Lion of Judah to arise in _____ this hour; _____ will no longer cower down in fear but arise to his God given destiny. Where there have been chains of bondage, they are breaking off right now in the name of Jesus. I thank you that the Lion roars again and when the Lion roars, all chains of debilitating doubt, fear and anxiety are broken.

I thank you that _____ has the boldness, strength and courage from Jesus alone, not pseudo boldness, strength and courage found in aggression, being a workaholic or being independent.

I thank you that _____ is fully able to accomplish all that God puts in front of his path.

I thank you that _____ is bold and full of courage in seeking out healthy relationships.

I thank you that _____ is bold, full of strength and courage in the ways of the Lord.

2 Timothy 1:7, NKJV

[7]For God has not given us a spirit of fear, but of power and of love and of a sound mind.

Pray for Men's Provision

Declare out loud the following scripture verses of blessed provision from **Deuteronomy 28:1–14** over _____ life. As you are declaring, insert _____ name (e.g. "Now it shall be _____, if you diligently obey the LORD your God, being careful _____ to do all His commandments which I command you today, the LORD your God will set you, _____, high above all the nations of the earth. All these blessings will come upon you, _____ and overtake you, _____,).

Deuteronomy 28: 1–14, NASB

Now it shall be, if you diligently obey the Lord your God, being careful to do all His commandments which I command you today, the Lord your God will set you high above all the nations of the earth. ² All these blessings will come upon you and overtake you if you obey the Lord your God:

³Blessed *shall* you *be* in the city, and blessed *shall* you *be* in the country.

⁴"Blessed *shall be* the offspring of your body and the produce of your ground and the offspring of your beasts, the increase of your herd and the young of your flock.

⁵"Blessed *shall be* your basket and your kneading bowl.

⁶"Blessed *shall* you *be* when you come in, and blessed *shall* you *be* when you go out.

⁷"The LORD shall cause your enemies who rise up against you to be defeated before you; they will come out against you one way and will flee before you seven ways. ⁸"The LORD will command the blessing upon you in your barns and in all that you put your hand to, and He will bless you in the land which the LORD your God gives you. ⁹"The LORD will establish you as a holy people to Himself, as He swore to you, if you keep the commandments of the LORD your God and walk in His ways. ¹⁰"So all the peoples of the earth will see that you are called by the name of the LORD, and they will be afraid of you. ¹¹"The LORD will make you abound in prosperity, in the offspring of your body and in the offspring of your beast and in the produce of your ground, in the land which the LORD swore to your fathers to give you. ¹²"The LORD will open for you His good storehouse, the heavens,

to give rain to your land in its season and to bless all the work of your hand; and you shall lend to many nations, but you shall not borrow. ¹³"The LORD will make you the head and not the tail, and you only will be above, and you will not be underneath, if you listen to the commandments of the LORD your God, which I charge you today, to observe *them* carefully, ¹⁴and do not turn aside from any of the words which I command you today, to the right or to the left, to go after other gods to serve them.

Pray for Men as Providers and for Jobs/Finances

Men all too often feel the immense pressure from society that they must fill the role of providers. I would go as far as stating to feel so is inherently in their DNA from birth. So here it goes ... please note I am not oblivious to the fact of the twenty-first century roles in a family, (even as I write this I am single and the sole provider). God is the ultimate provider. This is a book for women praying for men, so that is the view on which I am focusing these prayers.

Prayer:

As _____ provides for our/his family, I pray that God's hand of favour would be on _____ life in this area. I pray for favour with _____ employer (or employees), the government, the banks, policy makers, co-workers, etc. I pray that _____would have renewed energy every single day he goes to work and that work would be more than a mundane cyclical pattern, counting down the days until retirement. I pray that every single day will be full of passion, where God is going to use _____ in a powerful way in the everyday. I thank you God, that you have entrusted _____ with gifts and talents to be used in the workplace that will bring you, God, honour and glory. I thank you that _____ has desires and passions that you want to fulfill in his area of work. Restore the passion of why _____ is doing what he is doing.

I pray against weariness, tiredness, defeat and complacency. As _____ is working, I pray that you give him zeal as a provider. However, place it on his heart that God is the ultimate provider. I call forth _____ as a co-labourer with God. _____ has the Holy Spirit living inside of him, therefore he can and will accomplish every challenge set before him on his job with demonstrations of the fruit of the Spirit: "love, joy, peace, patience, kindness, goodness, faithfulness, gentleness, self-control . . ." **Galatians 5:22, NASB.** _____ will not compromise in his area of work no matter how tempting the payoff appears. _____ is set with a heavenly perspective and does not give into lusts of the flesh. _____ conduct on the job is a representation of the character of Christ. _____ experiences abounding grace in the area of his job, people are drawn to _____, as he is the light of Christ:

"Let your light so shine before men, that they may see your good works, and glorify your Father which is in heaven," **Matthew 5:16, KJV.**

Prayer specifically for men in need of a job:

I thank you God that your hand is on our economy and our government. I pray forth creative ideas, even entrepreneurial spirits to fall on _____. I pray for his motivation to not lack in the area of finding work. I pray for timely, godly appointments and connections, I pray for clarity on the next steps that _____ is to take in finding work. Open up doors that need to be opened and close the doors that are not from you. I pray against any hope that would be deferred in this area. I speak life over this situation and I give you thanks and praise for the provision you already have for _____ and this/his family. I thank you that you are working on _____ behalf already, even if we do not see it with our natural eyes. I thank you that you are a God of the supernatural and your thoughts and ways are above ours. I pray for a steadfastness, courage and confidence that does not diminish during this time. I pray for a boldness to fall on _____; speak to his heart if he needs to take specific courses, go back to school, change locations or take risks during this season. I thank you that during this season you are the ultimate provider. _____ identity does not come from a title, a job, or a certain

49

amount of income, but _____ identity is rooted deep in Christ and it is unshakeable; he lacks nothing being rooted in Christ. _____ is a child of God and an heir to the kingdom of Heaven. I thank you for your continued grace and more grace during this season; I thank you that God's provision during this time would be a testimony of your goodness and faithfulness on _____ life. I thank you that you are showing up in creative ways to bless _____ family everyday as a reminder to him and many others that God is our supplier and source, not money. Just like you provided for the Israelites in the desert so their shoes and clothes never wore out and gave them food for forty years from heaven, you also provide for _____.

Below are a few encouraging scriptures to speak out and declare as promises over _____.

Matthew 6:26, NASB

Look at the birds of the air, that they do not sow, nor reap nor gather into barns, and yet your heavenly Father feeds them. Are you not worth much more than they?

Philippians 4:19, NASB

And my God will supply all your needs according to His riches in glory in Christ Jesus.

Matthew 6:31-33, NASB

[31] Do not worry then, saying, 'What will we eat?' or 'What will we drink?' or 'What will we wear for clothing?' [32]For the Gentiles eagerly seek all these things; for your heavenly Father knows that you need all these things. [33]But seek first His kingdom and His righteousness, and all these things will be added to you.

Study God's name, Jehovah Jireh and begin to call God by who God himself says he is.

"Jehovah-Jireh" is one of the many different names of God found in the Old Testament. "Jehovah-Jireh" is the KJV's translation of YHWH-Yireh and means "The LORD Will Provide" (Genesis 22:14). It is the name memorialized by Abraham when God provided the ram to be sacrificed in place of Isaac."[3]

---

3 What does it mean that God is Jehovah-Jireh?; Got Questions; CEO, S. Michael Houdmann; https://www.gotquestions.org/Jehovah-Jireh.html. Accessed July 2017.

Prayer for Finances:

We thank you God for finances! I pray that _____
is a wise steward and leader in the area of finances. I thank
you that _____ is a lender and not a bor-
rower. I thank you that _____ gives the tithe
first and is generous, especially to the poor; direct him in
his area of giving. I thank you that _____
makes wise investments and uses his money as directed by
God. I thank you that _____ does not have
a spirit of poverty and if he does have a generational line
of poverty, I declare that it is cut off in the name of Jesus.
Pray **Deuteronomy 28:3-14, NASB** over _____,
this scripture can be found under "Pray for Men's Provision".

Now I encourage you to come up with your own prayer
for _____, offering him specifically what he
needs at this time. The list below might help to trigger a
need and if you do not know his needs, why not ask him?
The men for whom you pray might need help with:

- Asking for favour with a co-worker or boss

- Asking for a promotion

- Changing jobs

- Acting on opportunities to minister at work

- Wanting friends at work

- Finding himself overloaded at work

- Moving locations

- Combating a lawsuit

- Contemplating going back to school or switching professions

- Starting his own business

- Requesting a favour from the bank

- Wanting more hours of work

- Wanting fewer hours of work because of needs with his family

- Building confidence in bringing forth new ideas and sharing talents

- Facing a company that is experiencing layoffs

- Needing to confront his boss

- Overcoming a workplace injury

Pray for Men as Spiritual Leaders in the Household, Society and Church

I call forth men to arise as the leaders in their household, society and Church. I give men permission to have God given authority over the family unit and Church. Brave, uncompromising men will lead the home, society and Church in the ways of the Lord. These men will continually be developing in godly character and bearing witness to the fruits of the Holy Spirit. These men will be a great witness for generations as to how God has restored men in the home, in society and within the Church.

Prayer:

Arise out of the shadows you mighty men of God and take your rightful place within the home, society and Church. I stand against any attack of the enemy on a man's worth, value and gender role (as taught by the scriptures), I do not cower down to the enemy in the face of societal popular opinion, but I stand firm on the word of God, the Bible; men will be leaders once again.

I declare that, yes, men are needed in the home, society and family. _____ rise up.

I declare that men are needed in the Church as leaders. _____ rise up as a leader in the Church.

I declare that men's godly examples are needed in the Church, society and family. _____ rise up as a godly example in the Church, society and family.

Read over the fruit of the Spirit below and call out the fruit of the Spirit being activated in _____ life as a beautiful, representation of Jesus in the home, society and Church, providing godly leadership and a living example. The Amplified version gives what most of us are used to hearing; however, really take the time to let the message version sink in to the depth of what type of leadership you are calling forth in these men and the impact it will have on the home, society and Church if men begin to walk out as leaders in the fullness of everything the Spirit has put on the inside of them. Just start thanking God for giving _____ the fruit of the Spirit.

Galatians 5:22–23 Amplified Bible (AMP)

[22] But the fruit of the Spirit [the result of His presence within us] is love [unselfish concern for others], joy,

[inner] peace, patience [not the ability to wait, but how we act while waiting], kindness, goodness, faithfulness, [23] gentleness, self-control. Against such things there is no law.

Galatians 5:22–24 The Message (MSG)

[22]But what happens when we live God's way? He brings gifts into our lives, much the same way that fruit appears in an orchard—things like affection for others, exuberance about life, serenity. [23]We develop a willingness to stick with things, a sense of compassion in the heart, and a conviction that a basic holiness permeates things and people. We find ourselves involved in loyal commitments, not needing to force our way in life, able to marshal and direct our energies wisely.

[24]Legalism is helpless in bringing this about; it only gets in the way. Among those who belong to Christ, everything connected with getting our own way and mindlessly responding to what everyone else calls necessities is killed off for good—crucified.

E.g. Below is **Galatians 5:22–24** modified so you can declare over and thank God for the men in your life. Note: insert specific men, your husband, son, nephew, uncle, dad, neighbour, friend, etc. into the blank spaces.

Prayer:

I thank you that _____ lives God's way! I thank you that _____ has the gifts of the fruit of the Holy Spirit, that _____ is affectionate towards others, _____ has an exuberance about life and _____ has serenity. _____ has a willingness to stick with things. _____ has a compassionate heart and a conviction of holiness. _____ is loyal in his commitments and he does not need to force his way in life. _____ is able to marshal and direct his energies wisely.

Pray for Men's Physical Health

I thank you for the physical manifestations of healing taking place in _____ body.

I felt led to write down these specific diseases. However, know that God, Jehovah Rapha[4], is a healer and if the disease is not listed here, add it in:

Skin conditions

Eye diseases

Immunity

Fatigue

Migraines or head trauma

Joints

---

4 "Rapha is a Hebrew word meaning **"to restore" or "to heal"**. Therefore, the name Jehovah Rapha can be translated to mean "The Lord who heals". This name reveals God's aspect as a healer who heals people's spiritual and physical needs".

Which Aspect of God Does Jehovah Rapha Represent?; Reference; IAC Publishing, LLC; https://www.reference.com/world-view/aspect-god-jehovah-rapha-represent-d64e10c47f7eea8. Accessed February 2018.

Diabetes

Cancers

High Blood Pressure

Prayer:

Every disease and infirmity must bow at the name of Jesus. Jesus' blood is full of life. _____ is under the blood of Jesus. I speak to every cell in _____ body to come alive and function the way it was designed to operate. I speak life, health and wholeness. I speak to (name the disease) and declare that it is gone in _____ body. _____ body has to come into perfect alignment with the will of Jesus. (Name the disease) has no more authority over _____ life, _____ will no longer miss work, sleep, family time or worry over finances or be at a loss of joy or peace because of (name the disease). I break off any unforgiveness or family blood line where the (name the disease) could have entered. I close every door and bind up any attack from the enemy over _____ life. Everything stolen from _____ during this illness will be returned to him one- hundred fold. I speak peace, peace, joy, joy, energy, energy, zeal and more zeal over _____. God always gets the final word and the final verdict is (name the disease) has to go; all spirits of infirmity have to leave; an eviction notice is made today in _____ body!

The Bible is full of scriptures about Jesus healing the sick. I have recorded a few below. You can also go and do your own Bible study. Grab hold of these scriptures and start to speak truth from the word of God over _____ life. Remember the promise from **John 14:12–14**.

John 14:12–14, NIV

[12]Very truly I tell you, whoever believes in me will do the works I have been doing, and they will do even greater things than these, because I am going to the Father. [13]And I will do whatever you ask in my name, so that the Father may be glorified in the Son. [14]You may ask me for anything in my name, and I will do it.

Isaiah 53:5, NKJV

[5] But He *was* wounded for our transgressions,
He *was* bruised for our iniquities;
The chastisement for our peace *was* upon Him,
And by His stripes we are healed.

Matthew 9:35, NIV

Jesus went through all the towns and villages, teaching in their synagogues, proclaiming the good news of the kingdom and healing every disease and sickness.

Mark 5:34, NIV

He said to her, "Daughter, your faith has healed you. Go in peace and be freed from your suffering.

Luke 8:49–56, NIV

[49]While Jesus was still speaking, someone came from the house of Jairus, the synagogue leader. "Your daughter is dead," he said. "Don't bother the teacher anymore." [50]Hearing this, Jesus said to Jairus, "Don't be afraid; just believe, and she will be healed." [51]When he arrived at the house of Jairus, he did not let anyone go in with him except Peter, John and James, and the child's father and mother. [52]Meanwhile, all the people were wailing and mourning for her. "Stop wailing," Jesus said. "She is not dead but asleep." [53]They laughed at him, knowing that she was dead. [54]But he took her by the hand and said, "My child, get up!" [55]Her spirit returned, and at once she stood up. Then Jesus told them to give her something to eat. [56]Her parents were astonished, but he ordered them not to tell anyone what had happened.

James 5:14–15, NIV

Is anyone among you sick? Let them call the elders of the church to pray over them and anoint them with oil in the name of the Lord. [15]And the prayer offered in faith will make the sick person well; the Lord will raise them up. If they have sinned, they will be forgiven.

Jeremiah 30:17, NIV

But I will restore you to health and heal your wounds,' declares the LORD...

Pray over Men's Hearts: No Depression, No Insecurities, No Shame and No Condemnation

Just as John wrote to Gaius in **3 John 2, NASB,** "Beloved, I pray that in all respects you may prosper and be in **good health,** just as your **soul prospers,**" we also when praying for physical symptoms of disease, recognize the link between our soul and physical health, therefore we pray for the soul: our mind, will and emotions (all heart conditions).

I speak alignment of the scripture **Proverbs 4:20–22, NASB:** "My son, give attention to my words; Incline your ear to my sayings. Do not let them depart from your sight; Keep them in the midst **of your heart.** For they are life to those who find them and **health to all their body."**

Just a few scriptures to keep in your memory as you pray for _____ that offer health to his body; you can look up and write down more.

1 Peter 5:7, NIV

Cast all your anxiety on him because he cares for you.

John 14:27, NLT

I am leaving you with a gift-peace of mind and heart. And the peace I give is a gift the world cannot give. So don't be troubled or afraid.

Isaiah 54:4, NIV

Do not be afraid; you will not be put to shame. Do not fear disgrace; you will not be humiliated. You will forget the shame of your youth and remember no more the reproach of your widowhood.

Nehemiah 8:10, NLT

...Don't be dejected and sad, for **the joy of the Lord is** your **strength**!

Prayer:

Proverbs 4:23, NASB: "Watch over your heart with all diligence, For from it flow the springs of life." Lord,

I pray for _____ heart. I pray against all offense, strife, bitterness, envy, hopelessness, shame, doubt, etc. that has seeped into _____ heart. I thank Jesus that his blood is the healing balm rubbed all over _____ heart penetrating to the deepest heart wounds. I thank you for the restoration of _____ heart and the miraculous deliverances taking place right now in _____ heart. I thank you that _____ is his own diligent watchmen guarding his own heart from any attack of the enemy. **1 Peter 5:8, NIV:** "Be alert and of sober mind. Your enemy the devil prowls around like a roaring lion looking for someone to devour."

As the prayer above thanks Jesus that his blood is the healing balm of Gilead, I encourage you to do a Bible study on this healing balm and receive revelation on what it means; it is not just fancy words to add into a prayer. The following offers some insight.

"Is there no balm in Gilead?"

In three different places the Old Testament mentions the "balm" or healing ointment that comes from Gilead, the mountainous region east of the Jordan River. When Joseph's brothers conspired against him in **Genesis 37**, they sold him to a caravan of Ishmaelites from the region of Gilead carrying a load of gum, balm, and myrrh (v. 25).

73

Jeremiah 46:11 mentions the healing balm of Gilead. **Jeremiah 8:22** poses a question to the sinning people of Judah:

Is there no balm in Gilead?
Is there no physician there?

A well-known African-American spiritual applies the words of the text this way:

There is a balm in Gilead
To make the wounded whole;
There is a balm in Gilead
To heal the sin sick soul.
Jesus is truly the "balm of Gilead" for all the hurting
people of the world.[5]

---

5 Jesus is our "Balm of Gilead"?; Christianity.com; Ray Pritchard; http://www.jesus. org/is-jesus-god/names-of-jesus/jesus-is-our-balm-of-gilead.html. Published March 19, 2011.

Notes: performed as an African spiritual by artist such as: Paul Robeson, Mahalia Jackson, Rahsaan Roland Kirk, et al.

Original copy date is uncertain, some believe Washington Glass's 1854 hymn, "The Sinner's Cure".

Search and listen to the song through one of the footnotes
and sing it out over _____.[6]

6 There Is A Balm In Gilead- Deborah Liv Johnson; YouTube; beanscot; https://www.youtube.com/watch?v=BN9JALQRMb0. Published on Nov. 2, 2007.

Mahalia Jackson- There is a Balm in Gilead; YouTube; DaSourcespr06; https://www.youtube.com/watch?v=DFMY4V7RdbU. Published on May, 2008

'There is a balm in Gilead'; You Tube; Ronald Ellis; https://www.youtube.com/watch?v=8fcMxI_6xsk. Published on Aug 23, 2012

Pray for Men to make Jesus Lord of their Life in all Areas

I pray for _____ to make Jesus Lord of his life in every area. I give thanks and acknowledge that according to . . .

1 Corinthians 15:3–4 NIV

. . .Christ died for our sins according to the scriptures, [4]that He was buried, that He was raised on the third day according to the Scriptures . . .

And Revelation 19:16, NASB

[16]And on His robe and on His thigh He has a name written, "KING OF KINGS, AND LORD OF LORDS."

I thank you that _____ has revelation on that the way to the Father is through his Son, Jesus, only. I stand on the truth of . . .

John 3:16, NIV

[16]For God so loved the world that He gave His one and only Son that whoever believes in Him shall not perish but have eternal life.

I pray that nothing will claim first priority in _____ life over Jesus. Jesus will be exalted and our God glorified, based on the first commandment...

Matthew 22:37–38, NIV

[37]Jesus declared, "'Love the Lord your God with all your heart and with all your soul and with all your mind.' [38] This is the first and greatest commandment.

Jesus will not be left out of any area of _____ life. Jesus will be the center of all areas. _____ acknowledges that if someone is Lord over him, he is subject to obeying their commands, oh, how it is a great joy and honour for _____ to obey the Lord's commands.

Out loud make these decrees over _____ making Jesus the Lord of his life in all areas.

I decree right now from this day forward that _____ is making Jesus the Lord of his life over his finances.

I decree right now from this day forward that _____ is making Jesus the Lord of his life over his job/occupation.

I decree right now from this day forward that _____ is making Jesus the Lord of his life over his relationships.

I decree right now from this day forward that _____ is making Jesus the Lord of his life over his health.

I decree right now from this day forward that _____ is making Jesus the Lord of his life over his family.

I decree right now from this day forward that _____ is making Jesus the Lord of his life over his hobbies/talents.

I decree right now from this day forward that _____ is making Jesus the Lord of his life over his time.

I decree right now from this day forward that _____ is making Jesus the Lord of his life over his mind/will/emotions.

I thank you that _____ is putting aside his agenda, plans and will. _____ is partnering and aligning with the purpose and destiny God has for his life. _____ will fulfill with joy all that God has for him. _____ is surrendering entirely to the flexibility of the leading of the Holy Spirit, to bring God glory and thus, declaring yes, Jesus you are Lord of all in my life!

Pray for Men to Dream Again

I do not need to do a lot of convincing for you to believe that somewhere along this road of life, as little boys turn into men they have lost sight of their dreams and become complacent with their everyday, ordinary lives. Maybe it is the pressures of being responsible and providing; more work, less play. I have the privilege of being a Kindergarten teacher and it never fails when these five-year-old boys are asked, "What do you want to be when you grow up?", let me tell you, **the sky is the limit** and there is no telling them elsewise. I often hear firefighter, astronaut, policeman, scientist and yes, even super hero. I have never told any of the children, "No, that is just a foolish dream; let's get back to reality." At what point are dreams and the ability to stop dreaming, or do I dare say **believing,** come into play? I believe God has placed desires and dreams in us for a purpose and God is waiting in anticipation for men everywhere to start dreaming and believing once again.

Prayer:

I pray for _____ to be a dreamer; I thank you that you are stirring once again those desires/ dreams in him right now, in the name of Jesus. I thank you that you have placed God-given dreams inside of _____ and those dreams will be fulfilled in his lifetime. I thank you that _____ has a childlike spirit and faith. _____ is able to believe that the promises of God in his life will come to pass. I break off any doubt and fear in the name of Jesus. I thank you that no dream is too big for God; God is a God of the impossible.

Ephesians 3:20, TLB

[20]Now glory be to God, who by his mighty power at work within us is able to do far more than we would ever dare to ask or even dream of—infinitely beyond our highest prayers, desires, thoughts, or hopes.

Call out/decree the areas where dreams have been lying dormant in _____ life. Here are just a few to get you started; if _____ has other dreams, speak them out over him.

I thank you that business ideas are being birthed in _____ right now. There are millionaires/

billionaires, corporations, employers, inventions and new products being released right now.

I thank you that creative ideas are being birthed in _____ right now. There are writers, poets, actors, dancers, musicians, artists, inventors, etc. being released right now. I thank you for doors being opened right now.

I thank you that ministry ideas are being birthed and doors opened for _____ right now. There are missionaries, pastors, leaders, outreach workers, evangelists and prophets being released right now.

I thank you that governmental assignments are being birthed and doors opened for _____ right now. There are prime ministers, presidents, premiers, MLAs, MPs, senators, judges, mayors and ambassadors being released right now.

I thank you that godly fathers and spouses are being birthed and doors opened for _____ right now.

I finally call forth Christian men all over the world to be influential pillars in the seven mountains of society.[7] Stir

7 "In 1975, Bill Bright, founder of Campus Crusade and Loren Cunningham, founder of Youth With a Mission(YWAM), developed a God-given, world-changing strategy. Their mandate: Bring Godly change to a nation by reaching its seven spheres, or mountains, of societal influence."

The Seven Mountains of Societal Influence; Generals International; Cindy Jacobs; https://www.generals.org/rpn/the-seven-mountains/. Accessed August, 2018.

up godly dreams within them. I thank you that no dream is too big or small if it is God ordained. Thank you for all the teachers, policemen, lawyers, janitors, trades workers, accountants, military personnel, athletes, scientists and others that you are birthing out of dormant dreams being awakened in _____. I thank you that you are a God of purpose and every dream is God ordained and plays a part in the bigger picture. You do not just give a dream, but you make a way by ordering steps, opening/closing doors, changing hearts, attitudes and mindsets and putting words into actions.

I also want to pray over dreams as they sleep and over sleeping disorders.

Prayer:

I stand on your word as Joel in the Bible prophesied,

Acts 2:17, NIV

In the last days, God says, I will pour out my Spirit on all people. Your sons and daughters will prophesy, your young men will see visions, your old men will dream dreams.

I pray right now, in the name of Jesus, for God -given dreams to be awakened in _____ life as he sleeps. Just like Joseph and Daniel in the Bible were given dreams as they slept, I pray for _____ to also receive God dreams as he sleeps, dreams full of vision, direction and peace. I pray against any attacks of the enemy in the area of sleep. I pray and cut off nightmares in the name of Jesus. I pray against sleep depravation caused by anxiety and depression and irregular sleep patterns in _____ life. I even break off sleep apnea.

Psalm 127:2, HCSB
...He gives sleep to the one He loves.

I am sensing there even needs to be a breaking off of apathy in some of the men's lives. They have settled with the mundane and do not care anymore. Too many men simply go through the routines/motions, but find no real joy, only surviving and not really living life to the fullest. Their dreams are beyond stifled at this point.

Prayer:

I break off any apathy over _____ life in the name of Jesus. I declare that the Holy Spirit is igniting within _____ passion, life and purpose. Dreams are being awakened in _____ this very moment and apathy will no longer keep these dreams in paralysis. I declare awaken, awaken and awaken out of apathy _____!

I encourage you to sing out in declarations over
_____ the following song. This song carries
an anointing and the beginning lyrics are releasing life
and passion. Would you join in agreement with the lyrics
through song/declarations over _____ and
watch what the Holy Spirit does in his life? Even if you
need to have this song on repeat for one, two, three weeks
or a month, keep making declarations until you know there
is a shift happening over _____.

United Pursuit
"Let It Happen"
(ft. Andrea Marie)[8]

---

8 Let It Happen (ft. Andrea Marie)- Official Video; YouTube; United Pursuit; https://
www.youtube.com/watch?v=bvsAV-MgGao. Published on Aug 18, 2015.

Note: United Pursuit- Let It Happen is available for purchase on the Simple Gospel
CD from unitedpursuit.com

Pray for Men to take Positive Risks Once Again

These prayers are the sequels to the previous pages of, Pray for Men to Dream again. It is wonderful to have God-inspired dreams; however, if no action is taken, then that is all they remain, dreams. We believe for more in the lives of our men, so we are praying for them to take positive risks. Another term for what we request is to stir up their faith into action. Please do not undermine the importance of praying for the dreams, many men have become calloused and have blocked their brain from dreaming. One memorable quotation for me in school was, "Before the reality comes the dream," **Anonymous.** Hence, that is why we first pray for an activation of the dreams to be awakened again, so steps of faith can be manifested. Before we start praying take the time to read **James 2:14–26** (below) to fully grasp what the aim of this prayer is to stir up in our men.

James 2:14–26, NKJV

[14]What *does it* profit, my brethren, if someone says he has faith but does not have works? Can faith save him? [15]If a brother or sister is naked and destitute of daily food, [16] and one of you says to them, "Depart in peace, be warmed and filled," but you do not give them the things which are needed for the body, what *does it* profit? [17]Thus also faith by itself, if it does not have works, is dead.

[18]But someone will say, "You have faith, and I have works." Show me your faith without your works, and I will show you my faith by my works. [19]You believe that there is one God. You do well. Even the demons believe—and tremble! [20]But do you want to know, O foolish man, that faith without works is dead? [21] Was not Abraham our father justified by works when he offered Isaac his son on the altar? [22] Do you see that faith was working together with his works, and by works faith was made perfect? [23] And the Scripture was fulfilled which says, "Abraham believed God, and it was accounted to him for righteousness." And he was called the friend of God. [24] You see then that a man is justified by works, and not by faith only.

[25] Likewise, was not Rahab the harlot also justified by works when she received the messengers and sent *them* out another way?

²⁶ For as the body without the spirit is dead, so faith without works is dead also.

Prayer:

I thank you God that _____ is dreaming again, I thank you that you are imprinting godly dreams on his heart right now, in the name of Jesus. I pray that you would give him the blueprints of how the dreams are to be manifested in his life. I call down these blueprints from heaven in the name of Jesus. (There are blueprints for jobs, finances, business ideas, ministries, family planning, creative blueprints falling from heaven right now.) I thank you that _____ is obedient and hears from you Lord Jesus. Your word says that, "My sheep hear my voice, and I know them, and they follow me," **John 10:27, ESV**. I thank you that _____ is your sheep and he does hear and obey your voice/direction. Direct _____ in the tangible steps he needs to initiate right now to start activating his faith for the manifestation of this dream. I thank you right now that _____ is making the phone call, creating the resume, investing his money, mending that relationship, signing up for that course, phoning the bank, applying for that school or job, trying out for the team, or whatever course of action you are downloading on him right now in the name of Jesus. "Praise the LORD, you his angels, you mighty ones who do his bidding, who obey his word", **Psalm 103:20, NIV**. I thank you that angels are being dispatched right now with blueprints and are going before _____, opening up doors of great favour, aligning situations and preparing the way of the manifestation of these dreams to come to pass.

I pray over disappointments and failures of stepping out in the past that has caused great heart wounds in _____ life. I thank you that _____ past does not determine his future. "Hope deferred makes the heart sick, but a dream fulfilled is a tree of life", **Proverbs 12:13, NLT**. I bind up any hope that has been deferred and invite the Holy Spirit into _____ heart to start to heal and restore the wounds. I pray with expectancy and call forth many trees of life in _____ life as he begins to risk getting hurt again. _____ is fully equipped in the armour of God.

I thank you that these dreams that have been planted as seeds are growing deep within _____ until they become a full life-giving tree, bearing much, much fruit for the kingdom of God. I thank you that you are downloading wisdom on _____ right now. I thank you that you are making _____ bold as a lion, full of courage and confidence such that he will not cower down in fear to the lies of the enemy but will face every obstacle of fulfilling these dreams head on. He will accomplish what God has placed in his heart and sets before him now. I declare over _____ life right now that he is a mighty man of faith in God's eyes. His faith is not dead, because he is now being activated in the works set forth by God himself.

Pray for Men to have Male Spiritual Mentors

I call forth the male spiritual mentors to arise during this time on earth, as Kingdom culture is being brought down to earth. I call, awaken male spiritual mentors, awaken in this hour, month, season, awaken to the call of mentorship God has bestowed upon you, awaken past the excuses, come out of hiding male spiritual mentors for you have a much-needed voice, godly wisdom and profound insight to pass along to the men. No longer will the younger generations blindly try to navigate their way through this world, because spiritual Fathers have heard the call from the heavenlies and are awakening as mentors.

Prayer:

I thank you God that you have positioned _____ in a place where he will be surrounded by male spiritual mentors pouring into his life. I thank you that these are godly aligned relationships, hand picked by you, Father. I thank you that the spiritual mentors will pray, edify and pour into _____ life. These mentors will have godly wisdom of the supernatural and the natural realm and will be able to equip and teach _____ in the ways of the Lord in every area of his life. In turn _____ will arise himself as a male spiritual mentor, teaching and equipping men in this day of the ways of the Lord, both supernaturally and naturally.

This cyclical pattern of being mentored and becoming a mentor will be commonplace as men are being discipled, being brought up in the ways of the Lord. God has heard the heart cries of the hunger for men to arise during this time in the Kingdom and he is doing this through mentorship. So I stand with all men during this time on earth and declare that they are being awakened now to mentorship in Jesus name, Amen!

Proverbs 27:17, NASB
Iron sharpens iron, So one man sharpens another.

Proverbs 9:9, NASB
Give instruction to a wise man and he will be still wiser, Teach a righteous man and he will increase his learning.

Proverbs 13:20, NASB

He who walks with wise men will be wise, But the companion of fools will suffer harm.

Philippians 4:9, NASB

The things you have learned and received and heard and seen in me, practice these things, and the God of peace will be with you.

John 14:26, NKJV

"But the Helper, the Holy Spirit, whom the Father will send in My name, He will teach you all things, and bring to your remembrance all that I said to you.

Pray for Men to have Healthy Authentic Friendships with other Men

John 15:12–16, NIV

[12]This is My commandment, that you love one another as I loved you. [13]Greater love has no one than this, that he lay down his life for his friends. [14]You are My friends if you do what I command you.[15]No longer do I call you servants, for a servant does not understand what his master is doing. But I have called you friends, because everything I have learned from My Father I have made known to you. [16]You did not choose Me, but I chose you.

Prayer: The most important friendship is with Jesus.

I thank you that _____ is a friend of Jesus. _____ delights in the Lord and _____ is hungry to spend one on one time with the Lord: reading the word, studying, worshiping and resting in the Holy Spirit's presence. _____ has complete access to the throne room of Heaven because he is a friend. _____ has open communication with Jesus and is open to sharing his joys, fears, failures and successes with Jesus, because _____ trusts his friend completely. _____ puts his friendship with Jesus as first priority in his life, not trying to earn anything, but simply because he wants to. _____ does not look towards other humans, successes, or material possessions to fill a void in his life, because Jesus is at the center, filling _____ until overflowing with Love. All of Jesus' character rubs off on _____ because they spend so much time together; it is unavoidable and people take note of Jesus on _____ because he spends so much time in fellowship with Jesus. I thank you God that you have searched, chosen and wooed _____ into an everlasting relationship/friendship with you.

Prayer: Relationship with other Christians,

I thank you right now that you have and are continually aligning positive, male friendships in _____ life. These relationships will catapult _____ further into the fullness God has for his life. These male, Christian friendships are edifying, mentoring, holding accountable and bringing much joy into _____ life.

Prayer: Relationship with Non-Christians

_____ is impacting other non-Christian males, building healthy male relationships, although never compromising. _____ is a light.

Declare out the following scripture; say it, adding in the man's name to make it personal for him.

Matthew 5:14–16, AMP

[14] You are the light of [Christ to] the world. A city set on a hill cannot be hidden;[15]nor does *anyone* light a lamp and put it under a basket, but on a lampstand, and it gives light to all who are in the house. [16]Let your light shine before men in such a way that they may see your good deeds *and* moral excellence, and [recognize and honor and] glorify your Father who is in heaven.

Pray over Breaking Men's Sinful and Destructive Thoughts/Habits

Watch your thoughts, for they become words.
Watch your words, for they become actions.
Watch your actions, for they become habits.
Watch your habits, for they become character.
Watch your character, for it becomes your destiny.
-Anonymous

Luke 6:45, ISV

A good person produces good from the good treasure of his heart, and an evil person produces evil from an evil treasure, because the mouth speaks from the overflow of the heart.

Proverbs 18:21, NIV

The tongue has the power of life and death, and those who love it will eat its fruit.

2 Corinthians 10:3–5, AMP

[3]For though we walk in the flesh [as mortal men], we are not carrying on our [spiritual] warfare according to the flesh *and* using the weapons of man. [4]The weapons of our warfare are not physical [weapons of flesh and blood]. Our weapons are divinely powerful for the destruction of fortresses. [5]*We are* destroying sophisticated arguments and every exalted *and* proud thing that sets itself up against the [true] knowledge of God, and *we are* taking every thought *and* purpose captive to the obedience of Christ,

Romans 12:2, NIV

Do not conform to the pattern of this world, but be transformed by the renewing of your mind. Then you will be able to test and approve what God's will is--his good, pleasing and perfect will.

Below are prayers, scriptures and a song to declare out loud over _____.

Prayer:

Depression, anxiety, fear, lust, unworthiness, lack of purpose, eating disorders, identity issues and all other strongholds of the mind are being broken and coming under the Lordship of Jesus Christ in _____ life. The mind will no longer be controlled by sinful and demonic powers. _____ mind is being renewed into the mind of Christ. I close any open doorways where the enemy has gained access in the past, whether through the eye or ear gates; what _____ watches, listens to and reads will align with God's best for his life. _____ will even lose the desires to watch, listen and read anything that does not line up with **Philippians 4:8.**

Philippians 4:8, NIV

Finally, brothers and sisters, whatever is true, whatever is noble, whatever is right, whatever is pure, whatever is lovely, whatever is admirable—if anything is excellent or praiseworthy—think about such things.

I especially sense that there needs to be a breaking off of migraines and mind control over certain individuals.

Prayer:

In the name of Jesus, men's minds are being set free and the physical manifested symptoms of migraines are being broken and placed under the blood of Jesus.

I also sense strongly that suicidal thoughts need broken.

Prayer:

I come against suicidal thoughts; spirit of death has no free reign here, no free reign here. I declare that the spirit of death and suicide needs to pack its bags. I break off any generational curse of the spirit of death and suicide. Spirit of life is breathing on _____.

Philippians 4:6–7, NLT

⁶Don't worry about anything; instead, pray about everything. Tell God what you need, and thank him for all he has done. ⁷Then you will experience God's peace, which exceeds anything we can understand. His peace will guard your hearts and minds as you live in Christ Jesus.

1 Peter 5:7, NASB

⁷casting all your anxiety on Him, because He cares for you.

John 14:27, NLT

²⁷I am leaving you with a gift—peace of mind and heart. And the peace I give is a gift the world cannot give. So don't be troubled or afraid.

Pray for the breaking off of condemnation (yes, God will convict us, however, condemnation is not of God), then read the following scriptures and start declaring them out over _____. Also sing the song, "Nothing but the Blood of Jesus" out over _____.

Prayer:

I thank God that he is a loving father and that he corrects those he loves, "because the Lord disciplines the one he loves, and he chastens everyone he accepts as his son," **Hebrew 12:6, NIV.** I thank you that because _____ is a son of God you are convicting _____ of any area he has to change in his thought patterns that are leading to sin and death. I also pray for protection where the enemy will try to use condemnation over _____. _____ is loved by God and is a child of God. I declare God's revelation of how much he is loved by God to outpour on him. _____ is cleansed from all sin, guilt and condemnation because Jesus died on the cross for _____. _____ is being dipped in the blood of Jesus and there can be no case or accusation that will stand against him in the courts of Heaven.

Romans 8:1, NIV

Therefore, there is now no condemnation for those who are in Christ Jesus,

1 John 1:7, ESV

⁷But if we walk in the light, as he is in the light, we have fellowship one with another, and the blood of Jesus Christ his Son cleanseth us from all sin.

Nothing but the Blood of Jesus with Lyrics - Robert Lowry

What can wash away my sin?
Nothing but the blood of Jesus;
What can make me whole again?
Nothing but the blood of Jesus. Oh! precious is the flow
That makes me white as snow;
No other fount I know,
Nothing but the blood of Jesus.

For my cleansing this I see—
Nothing but the blood of Jesus!
For my pardon this my plea—
Nothing but the blood of Jesus!

Nothing can my sin erase
Nothing but the blood of Jesus!
Naught of works, 'tis all of grace—
Nothing but the blood of Jesus!

This is all my hope and peace—
Nothing but the blood of Jesus!

This is all my righteousness—
Nothing but the blood of Jesus![9]

Declare freedom over the mind then read the following scriptures declaring them out over _____.

Prayer:

Speak freedom, freedom; all chains are falling off, mind of Christ, healing the mind. As _____ stands in the courtroom of Heaven, he is free, he is free, he is free and the final verdict is _____ is free! _____ thoughts are pure and holy, he is blameless before God. _____ will think on things above, things that are pure, noble, true and all things praise worthy because _____ knows his identity in Christ as a person who is free and he will begin to think and walk out his life as a free person in Christ. Amen!

1 Corinthians 2:16, NIV

for, "Who has known the mind of the Lord so as to instruct him?" But we have the mind of Christ.

---

9 Nothing but the blood of Jesus; Hymnary. org; Robert Lowry; https://hymnary. org/text/what_can_wash_away_my_sin. 1876

2 Corinthians 3:17, NIV

Now the Lord is the Spirit, and where the Spirit of the Lord is, there is freedom.

Pray over Men as Conquerors

Men are rising up as Joshuas and Calebs in this hour. We are praying for men to have a spirit like Joshua and Caleb's. There is a boldness and courage coming over men as they rise up in unity, putting on their armour, ready to fight and conquer their promised lands.[10]

---

10 "The Israelites lost their one and only chance to go into this Promised Land due to one main reason – fear, and lack of full faith and belief in the power of God to see them through.

They were too scared of the giants and kingdoms they saw in the Promised Land they were supposed to possess – and they did not have enough faith and belief in God that He could conquer and defeat these giants for them.

As a result, they lost out on the biggest blessing of their entire life."

The Story of Joshua And Caleb; Bible Knowledge.com; Bible Knowledge Ministries; https://www.bible-knowledge.com/joshua-and-caleb/. May 2017.

Note: But not Joshua and Caleb, they operated by a different spirit of faith and courage and they were the only two to enter the Promised Land out of all the original men.

Prayer:

I speak life, not death over every situation in
_____ life. _____, you are
more than a conqueror.

Romans 8:37, AMP

37Yet in all these things we are more than conquerors
and gain an overwhelming victory through Him who
loved us [so much that He died for us].

I call forth God's destiny over _____ life.
_____ is equipped to fulfill God's destiny
in his life. He is guarded from all attacks of the enemy.

Pray and visualize _____ with the Armour
of God on him.

Prayer:

I thank Jesus wherever this armour has been taken off
or damaged, represented in a spirit of weariness, a spirit
of giving up, no fight left in him. I decree the opposite;
I pray with Heavenly insight, I declare and speak what
God sees and says, _____ is a man of fight,
passion and zeal, a mighty warrior of God, well equipped
for every battle. I pray for the armour to be restored to
_____, brand new!

Begin to thank God for each piece of the armour being placed on _____ and secured. I sense and believe that as we are praying for this Armour to be placed securely on, men are already rising up as warriors, conquerors in Jesus' name. There is a mighty army of Christian men rising up in unity, backed by the armies of Heaven. Angels are going before these men.

Prayer:

All fear has to flee in Jesus' name; all failure has to flee in Jesus' name. _____ is rising up, rising up to his calling in Christ. No longer will chains of fear bind _____. I declare a breaking of chains in Jesus' name. _____ is well equipped to conquer the Promised Land, the symbolism of his promises in his life and bringing the body of Christ as a whole into its promised land.

Every mighty warrior has mighty armour!

Read **Ephesians 6:14-17** slowly and begin to visualize _____ picking up each piece of armour as you read over that piece and thank God for each piece.

Ephesians 6:12–17, BSB

[12]For our struggle is not against flesh and blood, but against the rulers, against the authorities, against

the powers of this world's darkness, and against the spiritual forces of evil in the heavenly realms. [13]Therefore take up the full armor of God, so that when the day of evil comes, you will be able to stand your ground, and having done everything, to stand.

[14]Stand firm then, with the belt of truth fastened around your waist...

visualize _____ putting on the belt of truth. Thank you God for _____ putting on his belt of truth.

. . . with the breastplate of righteousness arrayed . . .

visualize _____ putting on the breastplate of righteousness. Thank you God for _____ putting on his breastplate of righteousness.

[15] . . . and with your feet fitted with the readiness of the gospel of peace . . .

Visualize _____ putting on the shoes of the gospel of peace. Thank you God for _____ putting on his shoes of the gospel of peace.

[16] In addition to all this, take up the shield of faith, with which you can extinguish all the flaming arrows of the evil one.

Visualize _____ taking up the shield of faith. Thank you God for _____ taking up the shield of faith.

[17]And take the helmet of salvation . . .

Visualize _____ putting on the helmet of salvation. Thank you God for _____ putting on the helmet of salvation.

. . .and the sword of the Spirit, which is the word of God . . .

Visualize _____ picking up the sword of the spirit. Thank you God for _____ picking up the sword of the spirit.

Men are moving into their rightful, God -inheritance as conquerors.

I call forth the individual promises of God to manifest in _____ life.

1 John 4:4, NLT

But you belong to God, my dear children. You have already won a victory over those people, because the Spirit who lives in you is greater than the spirit who lives in the world.

Pray for Men to Come into Full Revelation of God's Love for Them

I am reminded of the song:

How He Loves Us by Kim Walker-Smith / Jesus Culture[11]

I encourage you to buy this song and let the lyrics sink deep within your spirit. Begin to sing this song out over the men in your life and prophecy/ decree God's love over them! As you sing, change the word **us** to **you** and **me** to **you**, etc. Remember you are singing over the men, choose one at a time to sing over: your dad, brother, uncle, husband, son, cousin and others important to you.

---

11 How He Loves Us-Kim Walker Smith/ Jesus Culture-Jesus Culture Music; YouTube; Jesus Culture; https://www.youtube.com/watch?v=JoC1ec-lYps. Published on Apr 5, 2008.

Note: cd/dvd available for purchase at jesusculture.org

Romans 8:31-39, MSG

[31-39] So, what do you think? With God on our side like this, how can we lose? If God didn't hesitate to put everything on the line for us, embracing our condition and exposing himself to the worst by sending his own Son, is there anything else he wouldn't gladly and freely do for us? And who would dare tangle with God by messing with one of God's chosen? Who would dare even to point a finger? The One who died for us—who was raised to life for us!—is in the presence of God at this very moment sticking up for us. Do you think anyone is going to be able to drive a wedge between us and Christ's love for us? There is no way! Not trouble, not hard times, not hatred, not hunger, not homelessness, not bullying threats, not backstabbing, not even the worst sins listed in Scripture:

They kill us in cold blood because they hate you. We're sitting ducks; they pick us off one by one.

None of this fazes us because Jesus loves us. I'm absolutely convinced that nothing—nothing living or dead, angelic or demonic, today or tomorrow, high or low, thinkable or unthinkable—absolutely *nothing* can get between us and God's love because of the way that Jesus our Master has embraced us.

Prayer: I thank you that you love _____ so, so, so much. I thank you that you have good plans and a purpose for _____. I thank you that you know _____ so intimately that you even know every hair on his head and every tear he has cried. I pray that you would penetrate _____ heart with your unconditional love, that _____ would know that he knows how much you love him and how much you fight for him. Yes, I declare that God the creator of the heavens and the earth fights for you _____. God is for you, God is for you, oh, yes, and God is for you _____! No sin, no mistake could ever separate you _____ from how much your father, God, loves you. I pray that when you feel abandoned or left alone by people and situations in this world that you will have the full revelation and be able to tangibly feel God's never-ending love upon your heart and life_____. God is not a far distant Father but he is waiting patiently to woo you into an intimate Father/son relationship with him. I decree now that the delay is over and _____ is being wooed into his rightful position as son, while all barriers and apprehensions are being broken. _____ is being flooded by the Holy Spirit's presence and is being washed in God's revelatory love. Wave after wave, after wave of God's love is consuming _____.

Pray over Men's Identity

Who You Are: "We NEED you FULLY YOU! When you have a revelation of **WHO God is** and WHOSE you are, you will have a revelation of who YOU are." Lisa Bevere[12]

Scriptures on understanding identity, know whose you are!

Speak the scriptures out over _____.

John 15:15–16, NASB

[15]No longer do I call you slaves, for the slave does not know what his master is doing; but I have called you friends, for all things that I have heard from My Father I have made known to you. [16]"You did not choose Me but I chose you, and appointed you that you would go and bear fruit, and *that* your fruit would remain, so that whatever you ask of the Father in My name He may give to you.

---

12 Bevere, Lisa; Facebook; https://www.facebook.com/lisabevere.page/videos/10158050994575447/. February 3, 2017

2 Corinthians 6:18, NIV

And, I will be a Father to you, and you will be my sons and daughters, says the Lord Almighty.

Ephesians 1:5, NLT

God decided in advance to adopt us into his own family by bringing us to himself through Jesus Christ. This is what he wanted to do, and it gave him great pleasure.

Genesis 1:27, NIV

So God created mankind in his own image, in the image of God he created them; male and female he created them.

Know who God is:

We need to know who Jesus is . . . seeing Jesus with a crown on, Jesus is already **KING**, ruling and reigning, not a baby in a manger anymore. We know the end of the book, the Bible. I encourage you to buy and listen to . . .

Natalie Grant - King of the World[13]

---

13 Natalie Grant-King of the World; YouTube; New Christian Music; https://www.youtube.com/watch?v=4K7kplxNM48. Published on Oct 14, 2015.

Note: Natalie Grant- King of the World available for purchase from nataliegrant.com

God's Names

God's names and who God is, this is so powerful to declare who God is (not who _____ is); we need a higher perspective!

Below is a list of names God is called by(just to name a few). I have a book with over 100.[14] Start decreeing and believing who God is in _____ situation.

For example:

Thank you that you are actively **Jehovah Jireh** in _____ life, forever and always.

Thank you that you are the **Alpha and Omega** in _____ life, forever and always.

Jehovah Jireh: My Provider

Jehovah Rapha: My Healer

Jehovah Raah: My Shepherd

Jehovah Shalom: My Peace

Jehovah Elyon: Jehovah Most High

El Shaddai: The all-sufficient One

Jehovah Shammah: The Lord is with me Always

Beginning and the End

Alpha and Omega

Great I Am

The Trinity, three in one

---

14 Hill, Hazel. Praying God's Word: Shippensurg, PA: Companion Press, 1992.

The Father, Son and Holy Spirit
The Everlasting
My Provider
Bread of Life
Wonderful Counsellor
My Friend
My Glory and the Lifter of my head
My Peace

Prayer over their Identity:

I thank you that _____ is a son of the Almighty. I thank you that _____ walks in God's kingdom with confidence. I thank you for the revelation that _____ is receiving right now that he is made in the image of God and that the potter, God, does not make mistakes. Speak out these scriptures over _____.

Genesis 1:27, KJV

So God created man in his *own* image, in the image of God created he him; male and female created he them.

Jeremiah 1:5, NLT

I knew you before I formed you in your mother's womb. Before you were born I set you apart and appointed you as my prophet to the nations.

I break off any label spoken over _____ life that does not align itself with the word of God and _____ God -given destiny. I break off, even if well intended, any labels that are not of God that were spoken in the past, present or future by teachers, parents, spouses, children, siblings, co-workers, pastors, coaches and others. I decree a new banner of identity over _____ life:

New Banner of Identity to Declare

"Beloved prince, who is fearfully and wonderfully made, a joint heir with Christ, seated in heavenly realms in Christ, prospering in everything you do and goodness and mercy will follow you all the days of your life".

Below are scriptures to help support the new banner of identity you are decreeing over _____.

Psalm 139:14, ESV

I praise you, for I am fearfully and wonderfully made.
Wonderful are your works;
my soul knows it very well.

Ephesians 2:10, NIV

For we are God's handiwork, created in Christ Jesus
to do good works, which God prepared in advance
for us to do.

Romans 8:17, NKJV

…and if children, then heirs—heirs of God and joint
heirs with Christ, if indeed we suffer with Him, that we
may also be glorified together.

Psalms 1:3, NASB

He will be like a tree *firmly* planted by streams
of water,
Which yields its fruit in its season
And its leaf does not wither;
And in whatever he does, he prospers.

Psalm 23:6, NKJV

Surely goodness and mercy shall follow me All the
days of my life; And I will dwell in the house of the
Lord Forever.

Isaiah 62:3, ESV

You shall be a crown of beauty in the hand of the Lord, and a royal diadem in the hand of your God.

1 Peter 2:9, KJV

But ye are a chosen generation, a royal priesthood, a holy nation, a peculiar people; that ye should shew forth the praises of him who hath called you out of darkness into his marvellous light.

Ephesians 2:6, NIV

And God raised us up with Christ and seated us with him in the heavenly realms in Christ Jesus

Pray for the Holy Spirit to Saturate Men with his Presence

2 Corinthians 3:17, NIV

Now the Lord is the Spirit and where the Spirit of the Lord is, there is Freedom.

Just begin decreeing the above scripture out over _____ life.

Prayer:

I give you praise that the Spirit of the Lord is moving upon _____ life right now. I thank you that _____ walks in all freedom! Oh, Holy Spirit I invite you in to consume _____ life.

Below is such a powerful song to sing and keep singing out over _____ life. I encourage you to look the song up if you are unfamiliar with it and sing it out loud as a declaration. Sing it like you mean it; trust that God is moving his Spirit over _____. Switch the lyrics to him, he, his, etc. Remember this is so the spirit moves on _____.

Jesus Culture
"Set Me Ablaze"
(feat. Katie Torwalt)[15]

15 Jesus Culture- Set Me Ablaze (Live/Lyrics And Chords) ft. Katie Torwalt; YouTube; Jesus CultureVEVO; https://www.youtube.com/watch?v=RRwcIFHbRg0. Published on Mar 18, 2016.

Note: Jesus Culture- Set Me Ablaze is available for purchase on the *Let It Echo* CD from jesusculture.com

Printed in Canada